PEOPLE, PLACES & THINGS

The Powerful Nouns of My Life

by Jim Farfaglia

ISBN-13: 978-1482345797

ISBN-10: 148234579X

For Julie

I'm still here –
on the hands and knees of my poetry –
finding my way.

Table of Contents

CHAPTER THREE   THINGS   page

EPILOGUE   IDEAS   page

CHAPTER 1

PEOPLE

Garden Angel

I raise my tender hand to yours,
weathered and warm,
and we walk through your garden,
as my life is beginning
and yours, ending.

It's a vibrant world:
everything reaching and wandering,
swelling and sprouting,
and somehow you and I,

born of separate lands
and silenced by separate words,
come to share this patch of earth

and to share a language of the soul,
which I will come to treasure
as my first communion:

you   welcoming me into your clan of happy farmers,
        who love the soil like it is their flesh and blood

and me   safe within the bosom of our family,
        learning to love everything alive.

Urgent Care

Your love for me
is as deep as my blood
reddening your handkerchief
pressing against my sliced knee;
your other hand clutching the wheel
as we speed through town.

Moments ago I was your third child,
your second son,
and only one of the many reasons
you rise and attack life each day.
Now I am the most important thing worrying you,
snaking through traffic,
cursing out the slowpokes.

I do not cry.
There will be time for that later,
when the doctor stitches an end
to your undivided attention.
But for now, everything is quite right:

Just you and me, Dad,
in the front seat –
the world keeping its distance,
the blood I'm losing
a fair price
for your exclusive love.

Stirring

The heat from a summer's day
settles heavy in this barn loft.
Bales of hay have held that heat
into the evening, giving off a stifling odor.
But I don't care –
I'm sleeping out with Tommy tonight.
The two of us growing up,
growing away from our families

and toward each other.
Tommy is lean and rugged
and so cocksure of life.
Being close to him is like
being him.

>   (Once, at a self-empowerment retreat,
>   everyone was required
>   to adopt a new first name.
>   I did not hesitate for mine.)

This windowless loft closes in on me
and I fear I may suffocate,
but I do not leave.
Tommy's brotherhood trumps the loft's heat
and draws me nearer,
until I am close enough to hear
and almost feel
his steady, certain breathing. Then,

though I never show…or tell,
Tommy becomes
my first love.

You and Me Against the World

Here, handing me a vinyl disk,
This is a pretty song.
And off you went –

a busy working mom,
no time to offer answers
to her questioning son.

No time or no words
to give meaning to so curious a gift?
Yes, the song *was* pretty:

a mother pledging her protection
from all that could rain down
upon her child.

Maybe you noticed, Mom,
how the world kept storming
and – unable to make it stop –

you offered what you could:
the shelter of that song.

Homerun

How strange
standing at home plate,
gripping this bat too tight,
thinking I should be back home, in the bleachers,
watching my older brother
knock 'em out of the park.

But here I am,
camp counselor shadowing my stance,
adjusting the angle of my bat,
feeding me all the lines Dad had tried
but I never understood

'til now.
This ballgame coach,
probably fresh out of high school,
who I imagine hits it like a pro every time,
trying to get me to do it
just once –

and something in his voice,
something in his persistence,
something in me
                      wild to be set free
crying out
Now is the time.

Afternoons, Sixth Grade

We'd stream into the classroom,
back from lunch and recess,
and as we settled in our seats

you would reach for your book –
the latest adventure you'd chosen –
and we'd dive right into the next chapter.

I would sit back in my chair,
tummy satisfied, legs happy
from a few laps 'round the playground

and my mind would float there in your words:
the story's hero always just about our age
and always bubbling with life.

Oh, how you read with expression,
how my imagination seemed fathomless,
and how those stories wash over my heart, still.

Piano Lessons

Your name escapes me
but my memories of you play on;
rising strong from my piano,
whenever I strike
certain noteworthy chords.

You wore too much of everything:
perfume that filled our living room
and lingered for days;
rings that made your fingers clink,
that accented the rhythms you drummed into our heads;
and your bold choice of dress,
that turned all eyes your way,
which pleased you.

You taught me a lot.
Songs like *The Darktown Strutter's Ball*
I still play today,
and my fingers have found a second home
atop the old eighty-eights.

But more than that, teacher,
you showed me, so early on,
how to fill my life with harmony:

Wear exactly what it is I love.
Walk into a room like I mean it.
And let every song I play tell my story to the world.

Early Intervention

Up and down the aisles I follow this mop,
moving through my after-school shift.
Knowing this job so well gives me plenty of time
to dwell on my teenage drama,
to pine for all I've been missing.

Rounding the baby food aisle I see them heading my way,
that mother with her strange child:
the two-year-old she dresses like Shirley Temple,
but with a wrinkled face and soulful eyes
of a sage.

I keep working my mop – keep moving –
and, from beyond my control, keep staring,
until this child's eyes catch mine,
begging me to come in –

but I scurry off,
weaving this mop away from my confusion,
pushing my life through another hazy day,

while my heart – still gazing into those wise old eyes –
turns up a clue
of what it is I've been missing.

Ode to Mama Cass

People still marvel at her voice
– yes, she had quite a contralto –
but what my mind can never shake
was how well *she* could –

with all her heft
draped in that psychedelic era,
so fully embodying her music –
while I sat tapping my foot

everything I felt
crammed into the big toe of my awkwardness,
watching someone
who seemed like the sore thumb of show business

have the time of her life.

Trade-off

I leave my new friend's dorm room,
leaping stairs two at a time,
the energy of connection racing
through my freshman veins.

Rounding the second flight
my eyes see, first, a pointed pistol,
then, your gangster-movie pose,
and, finally, your eyes, drugged and fearful

that see me as a narc,
ready to blow your cover –
not the shy boy
who lives too quietly down the hall.

And we freeze (thank God, we froze)
suspended in our separate but equal joy and fear.
And surely what saved me is the deal we silently struck,
swapping emotions on that stairway:

a smile spreading across your awakened face
and a crippling fear sidling up my spine,
where it found a home
and remains to this day.

Night Friend

On steps still warm from the August sun
we sit outside your cabin,
the night sky – like life –
just opening up,
and its many points of wonder
glimmering like the campers entrusted to our care.

It's heaven having a moment to ourselves,
our days so full and bright.
I don't have a clue how to manage kids
and I don't understand what it is I'm feeling,
but it's all pouring out of me now

like meteor showers over the lake:
my troubles tumbling onto unsettled waters,
your open heart, my lifeboat.

Why I Celebrate You

That harmony we created singing the big ballads:
Evergreen, Rocky Mountain High.
Oh, how we'd build to those powerful endings,
how they took us some place,
and how we never wanted to come back.

That Christmas we kept the tree up 'til March:
some nights camping out beneath it,
conversations drifting off,
our hope blinking blue and red
and yellow.

That crisp spring morning you challenged me to a foot race:
letting me keep your pace 'til we reached our street,
where you hit your stride,
rushing to the finish line,
there to greet me with a bear hug.

And all the other times, none eventful, perhaps,
but special in the way you matched my emotion –
note for note, hope after hope,
and because, in all the days before you and after,
no other man has ever done that.

For John Merrick, the Elephant Man

It was your outsides
that people condemned in horror
and cried over in pity.
But, with tender heart,
you struggled on.

It was my insides
that seemed just as hideous
and hardened my heart.
But, illumined by your footsteps,
I journeyed on.

Body Said to Be That of Stowaway Who Fell From Plane
USA Today   BOSTON   A North Carolina teenager whose body was found in a Boston suburb two days ago, had most likely stowed away inside an airplane's wheel well and fallen…

Released

True to an adolescent's logic
you found an inconceivable way to leave the nest.

Who knows if it was the cold, or the thin air,
or the release from that majestic bird's belly

that sent you free-falling,
so close to your re-beginning.

This world may never know the why of it all,
and yet my questful heart is already sure:

The urge to fly stirred, and you,
deaf to all those grounded voices, said yes.

Bestowal

To hell with the preachers and prophets,
the therapists, the authors!
They all wasted too many clever words
promising to make me whole;
none of them ever giving me all you did,
gentle caretaker:

Welcoming me to your retreat center
where I'd signed in, bound and determined
to weep my way out from under
the permanent cross I bore.
Somehow, in a weekend,
I would learn to accept myself.

And when you asked my reason for coming
(One more person who would shower pity on me?)
I was not prepared for your response –
trim and fit,
intriguingly vital,
the right road I would thereafter travel:

*Jim, you will someday find
that what you came here wanting to lose
is your greatest gift.*

Chorus Boy

You were easy to notice:
onstage amongst those chattering songbirds,
sitting in a chair of metal and wheels,
your body broken in ways I could not fathom.

And as your group found its harmony,
I was lost in my worry –
anguishing over the harsh reality
that, surely, was your denied life.

Then you sang your first note:

Rich and wholehearted,
your outstretched arms reaching us,
your eyes holding us bright,
for they saw what I could not.

As I sat in desperation,
wondering how to rescue such a tragic child,
you would be saving us all
in pure voice.

Lumps

Thank you, son,
for not being done with me,
for interrupting our *Good night-Sleep tight* routine
and for slowing the march toward your growing up.

At your request I re-enter your bedroom,
smooth the covers over your belly
and, as the game always went,
check for lumps:
each gentle poke to your ribs evoking giggles
that build to belly laughs,

that built your body strong
and our love, even stronger.

Thanks Dad,
you sputter,
I forgot how that goes.

So Not to Forget

I stand in my driveway
and, with a wave and a thumbs-up,
wish you well. Before me,
filling the space of your fading car,
I see what remains:

a grown-up daughter,
taking flight,
beginning that eight-hour drive that ends
at your new life;

an aging dad,
heading inside the home that held our collective dream,
that holds it still,
in its emptiness;

a skyful of snowflakes
holding off the coming dawn,
shrouding the turnstile of change
with its gentleness;

and this thing we call love,
now stretching thin across 500 miles,
but tender and life-giving
still.

Rebuilding a Deck with My Brother

The way the claw of our hammers
   rips open what for decades lay dormant.

The way the tape between your hand and mine
   measures the distance between us.

The way the saw intersects new wood
   and, this time, we go with the grain.

The way the bubble of the level sways
   and finally finds us a balance.

The way the screw turns a true path
   and draws us together.

Resounding

Because I mark time
by the music I have loved
and by the way our love slips
in and out of tune,
it hit me hard hearing Lennon on the radio today...

Remembering a young you
dancing to the Beatles,
romping through their hits:
skin flushed, eyes closed to the world,
and that smile, so rarely revealed.

Years later, he and Yoko
croon *Starting Over* from my kitchen,
and it drifts to the bed where I lie,
still warm from our first night together.
I hear your voice atop theirs
as you scramble our breakfast,
cracking open a new era.

And today it is his lullaby, *Love,*
a tender piano cradling its simple lyric.
Remember how I burned that song
to your birthday CD,
which I hope you took with you,
for keeping memories aflame…

Does he move you like he moves me,
here, at my flickering core,
where the only thing that makes sense these days
is that we tried.

CHAPTER 2

PLACES

Road

The thin line that it was –
just a thread of this world, really –
was my world

and each weave of that line
drew me deeper
into the fabric of country life:

patches of muck,
stitches of streams,
pockets of woodland.

I wore that life
like my favorite pair of jeans,
that held me just right

and hold me today,
as I witness our threadbare world,
gratefully tethered to that road.

I've Always Been Ready

I climb off the couch
and move to the footrest –
closer to the TV set

closer to those children
tending sheep in a field
where they met our Lady of the Heavens.

And when I could get no closer
I slipped into that movie
and found God, waiting for me.

Not in some solemn building
        but out where the earth opens,
not from the lips of lecturns,
        but whispered to my searching heart,
not here, amongst the non-believers
        but from where He called those children home.

Which is why, later that day,
I taped paper wings to my shoulders
and jumped off the couch, again and again,

practicing for the day I would be called,
to join those children of Fatima,
free to live in a land

where there is no disbelief.

Through the Back Room

Every farmhouse had one: a back room built
with unfinished walls and rough-wood floors,
with a tattered rug beneath a tarnished sink,

where tired farmers wrung their hands of muck and misery,
where a sweat-stained towel on a rusted nail
wiped another day from the brow of all he'd given.

Just inside the door, a mat held his boots
standing at attention, ready for the next day,
and for every day thereafter – for that was life…

And when I miss it so, when I forget its simple truth,
I call on my dreams to take me back,
and when they do, I always enter

through that back room.

Muckland Meditation

It was there I learned the word endless…

Plowed fields as far as the eye could see
and black with potential.
I was born a dot on that earthen map
and navigated its richness, row by row.

Blue sky matched the muck's vastness
and its canopy lovingly "had my back"
as I came to trust the sky's sun and rain
and stillness.

An occasional bird called out,
pecking through that silence;
each treetop melody adding a new voice
to my beginnings…

Those songs cradled my youth,
and, from there, I grew strong and vital,
from there, I took the fertile soil of my childhood
and farmed myself a good life.

The Record Store

To get there I had to dodge the Rough Boys
who knew, too easily,
how to get at my heart.
So I went the long way,
driven by fear,
and guided by a radar for danger.
But it was all worth it,

to once again
flip through those discs,
hearing each 45 hit the next, like a heartbeat.

Finally, I'd choose one,
hand over a dollar
and slip that song under my coat,
covering my heart:
armor for the journey home.

Social Studies

Back row, in the corner.
Two desks, side by side.
Each day my curious knee meeting
your welcoming thigh.

So this is what all those love stories are about,
I realize, but never say to you
or anyone,
for that was our lot in life,

we wingless birds,
confined to a back-row perch,
while love was sung by other,
luckier souls.

Funny, though, how years later
I still feel our melody –
passing like a love note
from knee to thigh,

pulsating with its undeniable rhythm –
composed in the corner of Social Studies class
where you and I
wrote a history of our own.

Touring the Motown Museum

Am I really here?

Walking these hallways of yestersong.
Climbing the stairways of remembrance.
Standing in the same room where they once stood:

    The skinny, spinning Temptations.
    The passionate, pleading 4 Tops.
    Those playful and sultry Supremes.

All crowded in this living room dubbed their studio:
its furniture pushed to the walls, rugs tucked under couches
and, center stage, one dutiful microphone

capturing those Motor City songs
that powered my adolescence,
that traveled from this tiny room to my turntable,

where they swelled the small-town borders of my heart.

Camp Treasure

I turn my bike from this dirt driveway
onto a tree-lined country road,
heading home.
Last day of working summer camp
and I'm carrying all my belongings:
tattered T-shirts, a crusted bar of soap,
a few rocks from the beach,
and this enchantment with the world
I did not start the summer with.

Tears rise
and the road ahead becomes unclear.
I'm heading home, yes,
but home is not home anymore,
just like I am no longer me.
The awkward high-school kid
has discovered a part of himself
and, like a new friend,
I can't bear leaving camp without him.

So I pack him with my belongings
and ride away, listening to him
still washing in waves through my veins,
still exploring the deep forest of my soul,
still aglow in the campfire of my heart.

Lake Reflection

Most days we speed by you
on a heavily-traveled highway,
anxious to arrive at our busy lives;

the gentle curves of your shore
and the depths of your blue
lost behind buildings and billboards.

Now and then a boat moves over you
and a few birds still swoop by,
but no one swims in you anymore...

Back when we did, you knew just how to soothe
our steamy July days; your brisk waters
awakening our spirits...

Somehow, I had forgotten all that,
until tonight, walking your shoreline
and my friend suggests *Let's stop.*

In the quiet, we stand and face you,
the strained sounds of the highway fading
and, slowly, that goodness of you

     resurfaces.

Ode to Lake Effect

I've lived in warmer climates
and I remember surviving *their* winters:
elbows on the windowsill,
face atop pensive fists,
watching fluffy promises of snow float by
empty-handed,

knowing to my core
what January was supposed to look like:
the world rewritten in white,
every blanketed tree and bush
beckoning me

to pile on extra layers,
to walk among a million flakes,
to lose myself in a blinding blessing
that only a few
– here, in our stretch of the world –
ever receive.

The Hill

You,
in front,
eight years old.

Me,
cradling you,
thirty-something.

Our sled,
beneath us,
newly purchased with hope.

Daredevil's Run,
dropping straight down,
a legendary adventure whose time had come.

Halfway down you scream: *Stop!*
And I, wanting the same,
but knowing all too well,
offer nothing...

Did you feel the fear surrounding that silence?
Did my grip around your waist, meant as protection,
                    wrap you in trepidation?
And did you come to know life apprehensively,
                    as I have,
unlike other, luckier sons,
whose fathers threw their heads back and, at life,
                    laughed?

Where I Was Friday

Where I Was Friday
    Interoffice
    To Do List
    Board Mtg
    Voicemail
    Spellcheck
    BlindCopy

Where I Was Saturday

quiet

wide open fields

lungfuls of fresh air

the probing knock of woodpecker

snowdrifts reaching for evergreens grazing uncharted heights

Looking Into Retirement

I stand a long time on this bridge,
watching the river rush beneath me,
churning and quaking.

What a busy journeyman you are.
Why are you always in such a hurry?

I've asked that question of speeding cars,
of people at crowded malls,
and of myself.

Now I ask you.

A slab of ice rides the current in,
then out of view;
evidence that something upstream
– something bound, but restless –
was ready to be released

and now sails to its destination,
where it will bob in balmy waters
and thaw into my answer.

Florida Send-off

On the last day of my vacation
I witness the beginning
of someone else's adventure,

not through a TV screen,
nor from some internet live-cast –
neither could match the wonder

of our gathered group of hopers,
eyes raised to the night sky,
our silent prayers propelling that rocket on.

The Waves of Costa Rica

Two days into this vacation
and already the waves have personality;
each offering something to my desiccated spirit.

A few lap at the shore
like doctor-ordered lullabies,
pacifying my hardrock life.

Others roll in
like right-on-schedule freight trains,
waking the sleepy village of my yearning.

Then come the big ones
that hit like bombs, exploding my complacency,
reminding me why I'm here –

why a settled life
must sometimes be blown apart
for it to be discovered anew.

Battlefield

Evening settles in as scheduled.
Oprah chats with some famous person.
My latest harvest cools at the table.

Then, from the backyard,
rises a forbidding cry
and I rush to my window to find

the neighborhood dog,
with a baby groundhog in his mouth,
and their tug-of-life ensuing

then ending
by the dog's shake of his head *No*
with all the *Yes* that he is

and his conquest
laid at the end of this backyard battle
like one fluffy comma

which makes me pause –
all within
that has ever fought for my life

paying attention.

Garden Report

No sign yet.

Just the mound of dirt I dug up,
slipped you into,
sprinkled with a handful of rainwater
and proclaimed your home.

I stop by every day,
say my version of a prayer
and pull a few jealous weeds
snaking toward you.

You are nothing yet but my hope –
which means you are everything.
I gladly dream of the day
I will stop by and see

your first tiny hand
waving hello,
your green
all the riches I need.

CHAPTER 3

THINGS

Casper the Ghost

Oh, how I wanted you so!
How I imagined reaching through that TV screen
and gathering your friendly spirit

which I believed in,
believed was the answer
that would make all my dark questions
                                        vanish.

So there I sat,
your most loyal viewer,
waiting – on this side of a wish –
for you to appear.

Fruit

Funny how one word can change a life.

Before you spit yours at me
I was someone vital, pulsating –
someone living his word.

But after yours
I started questioning my vocabulary,
started redefining myself:

carrying schoolbooks cool-like, on the hip,
carrying conversations scripted, clique approved,
carrying my self, rhythm abandoned,
                                    marching.

Slippers

Each Christmas there'd be a new pair
and, by then, we'd be ready,
last year's threadbare
from all the comfort they offered.

She tried to vary the color from pair to pair
and sometimes there'd be a five-dollar bill
snuck in the toe,
but the color or the money never was the gift…

I got my last pair when I was twenty
and held onto them like the wise adult I was trying to be,
using them sparingly,
darning and re-darning each hole in the heels.

And I'd take any color, this Christmas,
if I could,
calling back her tired hands
to work those needles,

stitching me into a softer life
where, once again,
a pair of slippers under the tree
tilted each new year to the good.

High Fidelity

Today's digital music holds nothing
compared to those timeless vinyl discs
that I once held –

each with a hole that fit them
neatly atop my turntable,
where they ran their life in circles
so that I might set upon them
a diamond needle – and listen

as my favorite tunes rose from those grooves:
each song just about three minutes long,
long enough to learn about life,
or hell raisin',
or how to mend a broken heart.

And the records I loved over and over?
They wound up with crackles and skips
that became a part of those songs,

flaws ingrained into each story
like my mishaps were etched into mine.

And whenever life got boring
I could flip one over
and try out the B-side,
inviting a new song into my circle,

letting it revolve around my world,
keeping good time –
a time worth remembering.

Portrait

It was a captured sunset on a raging sea:
buckets of red crashing into gray and white;
all that fire and froth matted and framed.

Heaven knows how it ended up in our living room –
my parents weren't much for garage sales
and they never set foot in an art gallery –

but it hung there for years,
looking down on us all
bobbing in uncertain waters,

but especially on my dad,
stretched out beneath it every night,
exhausted from the struggle to keep us on course.

Years later that painting drifted to my house,
which I grew to appreciate:
Dad's storm hanging over me

stirring my ocean of regret,
smashing apart what held our distance,
calling to the surface what I'd given up as lost.

Miracle in Fur

Of the five teachers gathered
I am the most distraught:
newly-hired, shy and unschooled
in civil disagreement.

At the first probing question
my stomach knots,
and each panicked breath
incites it to flare –

Then, into the room she slips:
willowy, whiskered and waving
a tail of confidence.
She parades past the others,

hops onto my lap,
curls against my burning belly,
and purrs me
into some kind of powerful peace.

Observance

I think it's a blind sparrow, you say,
drawing my attention.

In silence we witness this curiosity:
visionless, but aflight.

She's finding her way though, you decide.
I nod, in communion.

Salve

The six of them graze into my yard,
tender noses to the early-spring grass,
searching for the sustenance
our deep winter has denied them.

Different sizes, different shades of that comfortable brown,
and one, I notice, favoring a front leg;
hoof barely meeting ground with each labored step.
Wounded.

From one of winter's traps?
From some aspiring hunter?
From the catchall of life's sorrows?

When the others move on, she stays,
something in this space healing her.
I watch, feeling her warm my winter-heart;
then, taking a tender step,

I start the foraging of my day.

Crescent

Can I live slightly?
Like you, carrying all I need from this world
in my silver sliver of a cup?

Can I hold steady?
Like you, fearless of the approaching clouds
and their end-of-the-world rumblings?

Can I trust the heavens?
Like you, certain that my turn to nothing
will come back 'round to everything?

    You are my teacher.
    And, like a good student,
    I have so many questions.

Namesake

(*Farfaglia*, in Italian, is *butterfly*)

Your arrival was a gift –
setting up house so close
I could no longer think of you
as that beautiful winged creature
who would always be
just out of reach.

Heaven knows how your younger self
wormed its way into my office
and latched onto the underside of my chair,
or how I ever managed to free a minute
and notice you.

But, after our introduction,
it was a pure infatuation.

Then came the day I arrived at work
to find your sac,
still hanging by a single thread,
but hollow.
How I panicked – the nursemaid gone mad –
until, opening the shades to throw light on my urgency,
I found you against the window pane,
folding and unfolding.

You did not hesitate to hop upon my finger
and, when I raised my hand to the great outdoors,
you paused

giving me a glimpse
of who it is we are.

Grazing Buddha

That cow –
the one plodding through spring
and shit
and straw –
seems to not notice
how she sinks a foot deep
with each step.

She just keeps searching for the world's nourishment,
which might come from the hay
or the sunshine
or the way she moves through her day.

Dreams Die Young

How did they become one:
the larger-than-life heron
found dead on a quiet city street,
and that old Janis Ian song
recalled from my flightless days?

Their stories wove in and out of each other:
the regal heron,
so careful to keep its dreamy distance,
now forced to die amongst us commoners
and Janis' voice
sailing along the treetops,
Odetta's moans
pulling her back to earth.

Dreams Die Young, the song foretold,
but nothing of my life believed it,
'til a fallen heron gave that song its wings,
and carried me to its truth.

Kramer vs. Kramer

You are 23,
home for a visit,
and we watch this movie together –

you, for the first time, and me,
not since I was on the other side of fatherdom
and divorce's mysteries lay undisturbed.

That's a lousy ending,
you say,
I thought they were going to get back together.

And another piece of my parenting-heart breaks.

Poinsettia

Today begins the magic.

Today I become a nature god,
ensuring exact amounts of sunlight and darkness
for this simple potted greenery.
By Christmas Day
it will become a bright and brilliant red!

As I ponder this transformation
I think about my life
and how far from nature's spectrum I have faded:
overly dependent on overhead lighting,
hunched for hours at my computer…

What if I were to begin balancing *my* need for light and dark?
What routines, once so important,
would drop like spent leaves?
What richness would rise from my roots
and spread through my veins?

How bright and brilliant would my red be?

Role Model

I want to be like that snake,
who did not stir
when I lifted my watering can,
revealing him in all his seated glory.

I want to live like he does,
offering nothing
when the world callously prods him –
just the wordless whip of his tongue.

I want to curl around my truth,
and sit with it, so,
when the world wants from me,
only I decide yes or no.

Moment

Gently
I pull weeds
near new flowers

who smile their thanks
reaching out from rich soil
to offer joy on a spring platter.

The breeze has lost its winter bite
and birds weave in and out of a song.
The ground holds my knees soft and dry.

No thought on either side of this moment calls.

Photo of a Woman Watching Obama's Inauguration

Her hint of gray:
a solitary road
woven through the blackest of times.

Her reflective eyes:
vessels of history
brimming with troubled waters.

Her gathered hands:
cathedrals of hope
shrouding prayerful lips.

> She looks to the TV for her salvation.
> I find mine looking at her.

I Am

I am turning compost:
standing in front of bin # 3,
where sun, air, rain and my pitchfork
have performed a patient miracle.

I am sifting bucketfuls:
capturing sticks, squash stems and cat dung,
watching the best of what remains
return to the open arms of earth.

I am shoeless:
my feet, having borne a tired spirit,
step into this renewed earth
and toe its truth.

I am stripping off gloves:
weathered hands plunging deep,
grabbing fistfuls of moist memories,
digging my way back.

I am being the best archeologist:
one willing to be with
the dregs of life,
to draw from it, a rich history.

Shakers

They're all that's left now:
two Holstein ceramic figurines,
one salt, one pepper.
Some of their painted splotches have chipped
and there's an ear missing from one –
but still they stand, side by side,

the last of the cow art we once rounded up.

Remember how our love domesticated us,
how we thought we could milk the good life forever?
Remember how we laughed bellyfuls,
plopping a few cow chips on an uptight world?

But, one by one, that herd thinned:

Gone are the embroidered calves on dishcloth,
lost are the cow-family finger puppets,
retired is the calendar of cattle in backcountry poses.
What's left sits on my kitchen table,
nobody paying them much attention –

except me,
on those days when life is but an abandoned pasture
and I turn them upside down,
watching those two
sprinkle some joy on this world.

EPILOGUE:

IDEAS

Ashes (How I'll Go)

Throw me to the wind.
Let rise what is most certain,
let fall what has no meaning.

Release my desire, and free it
to search and find my dreams.
Meet me there, Love.

Curl in and about me
as we dance our exhilarating truth.
Weep joy as we marry.

I lived in this body as one,
and ever did it yearn.
Now, let me know *together*.

ACKNOWLEDGEMENTS

I am grateful to the following proofreaders for their keen eye and thoughtful advice:

Kathy Andolina
Karen Burke
Mary Ann Donahue
Carolyn Dougherty
Wendy Kaplan
Linda Knowles
Tom Long
June MacArthur
Vince Markowsky
Maureen Moriarty
Geri Seward
Mary Slimmer

And to the following establishments for their support:

Downtown Writers Center
river's end bookstore
the Valley News

About the Author

Jim Farfaglia is a former teacher and camp director. He grew up and still resides in rural Oswego County, situated near Lake Ontario in Upstate New York. His first book of poems, *Country Boy*, was a testimonial to his farming family and rural roots. He is also the co-author of *Camp Hollis: The Origins of Oswego County's Children's Camp* and the editor of *Harvest* and *I Live As a Cloud*, two collections of children's writing. His poems are featured in *the Valley News'* weekly column, Poetry Corner. Jim maintains a website at jimfarfaglia.weebly.com.

Made in the USA
Charleston, SC
08 March 2013